Badu's Bad Day

Tales
from the
Serengeti

Badu was a
particularly
miserable baboon,
who lived with a
particularly
enormous family,
whom he found
particularly
annoying.
In fact, his family was
the main reason
he was always so
grumpy.

Badu's family spent
most of the day
grooming and cleaning
each other,
for they could
not groom themselves.
Everyone **enjoyed**
being cleaned,
everyone, that is,
except
Badu.

CONSTANTLY
having his
mother and father,
sisters and brothers,
aunts and uncles,
grandparents and
anyone else

who happened to be

around, picking at

every last inch

of him, drove Badu

crazy!

"ALRIGHT, THAT'S ENOUGH!"

screeched Badu one day. "Not one more pick of a tick can I take! I'm leaving! Don't worry about me. I'll be just fine, as long as you all keep your hands to yourselves."

"Okay," the troop meekly said and they all backed away. Then, without another word, Badu **bounded** down from the rocks of his home and escaped to a lonely, old baobab tree a short distance off.

"This is much
better already,"
Badu smiled to himself
as he relaxed
and scratched at a
small itch
on his back.
"From now on, I'll
just eat, sleep, and
do as I please!"

The next day was
quiet and *peaceful*
just as he had planned,
and more of the same
followed after that.
Now the only
thing that changed
as the days slowly
passed by, was the
small itch
on Badu's back
that seemed to be
growing
quite LARGE.

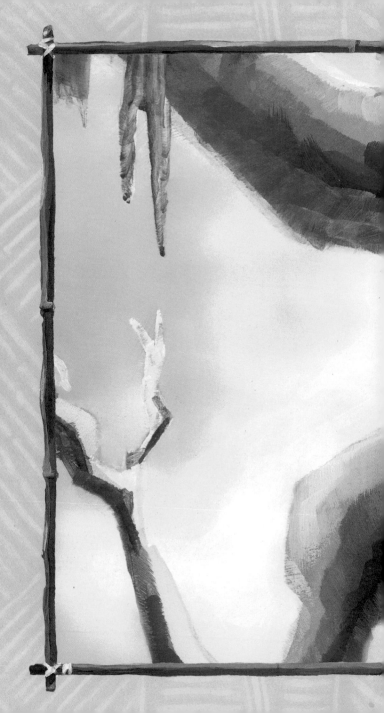

"It must be this **bRANCh**," he grimaced one morning. "No, this **tRee** is the cause. I'll just have to find a new home so I can be free of this **itching**."

A spotted hyena was
laughing
as she was passing by.
"I'll give you a hint,"
she snickered.
"It's not the tree that is
causing your distress,
rather a condition found
much
closer to home."